Roger Clark

PORTRAIT OF A GREAT RALLY DRIVER

Foreword
by
Roger Clark

David Campbell

 Publishing

First published in 1990 by
ghk Publishing
74 Esmond Road
London W4 1JF

© *ghk* Publishing

ISBN 1 873179 00 6

Main photograph selection: Colin Taylor Productions
Set in Palatino 10/12 point
Printed in Great Britain by Ashford Colour Press, Gosport, Hampshire

Contents

Acknowledgements

The research and writing of this book have left me with a great many people to thank for their help and advice. If I've left anyone out, I hope they will forgive me.

First of all, Tony Mason. Not only is Tony a great example — his energy and enthusiasm for rallying, even after all these years, are infectious — but it was he who convinced Roger Clark of the whole idea of a book in the first place.

My publishers, Bryan Kennedy and Gerda Holmsteen Kennedy, have put a great deal of time and effort into the book, and to them I wish to convey my heartfelt appreciation for their patience and understanding, even after the fiftieth missed deadline!

Paul Fearnley of *Motoring News* spent many hours researching results and statistics; and his boss David Williams, a true friend and mentor, was always on hand with advice and encouragement.

Adam and the two Chris's at Colin Taylor Productions deserve a special mention too. It must have taken hours to sort out all the photographs.

Every author has a long-suffering wife, and I am no exception. Amanda probably contributed more to this than she could ever imagine; to her my thanks and love. And to her parents, Maurice and Sylvia, sorry about the late nights!

Lastly — but not at all least — to Roger Clark: thanks for your time, patience and generosity, and for being such a worthy personal hero of mine. There could be no better subject for my first book.

David Campbell
September 1990

FOREWORD

Working on this book with David has forced me to look back on a large part of my life. And I have to say that I did so with pleasure. I feel very lucky to have had the opportunities and the good fortune to go rallying, largely at other people's expense!

I've often been asked which rally gave me the most satisfaction, and the answer is not what most people expect. It wasn't either of my two RAC wins, thrilling though they were. It was actually hauling that Rover 2000 around the Monte Carlo Rally to sixth place in 1965. That gave me a great sense of achievement. Beating the big Citroens (although they got their own back on me a year later!) and coming up with the goods for Rover were the big thrills for me.

My days at Ford were exciting too, of course, and I don't think anyone has any doubts about which car I liked most in rallying. They were good times, and we all had a great deal of fun together.

I look at Matthew now, and I see in him the same personality traits as myself. I don't know whether that's a good thing or not! Although the cars have changed dramatically, starting out in rallying seems to be much the same now as it was in my early days, and Matthew is doing it by himself, just as I did back in 1959. If he gets half the breaks I did, I know he will be very happy and successful. I certainly hope so, but I'm not one to interfere. It's all up to him now.

I still enjoy driving now and then, doing bits and pieces like the Pirelli Classic Marathon and the occasional historic rally. But I get more of a kick these days out of watching Matthew. It's uncanny how it reminds me of my own first steps in rallying. Perhaps I'm just trying to relive my own youth!

I hope this story of my rallying career is interesting to you. It's been a lot of fun for me, and if I had my life to live over again, I wouldn't change any of it.

Roger Clark
September 1990

Above: Only slightly sideways, Clark powers his Escort through a spectator stage on the 1972 Daily Mirror RAC Rally.
Below: "What's that over there?" Mason: "I think it's Stig parking his Saab on a park bench". Stig Blomqvist chased the British pair hard, but a lapse of concentration on a spectator stage which crashed his Saab into a bench didn't help.

THE FIRST MILESTONE

Deep in the forest of the Lake District, a small band of people gather at the edge of a gravel track. They stand together, rubbing their hands, pulling their collars in tight against the cold on a dark and damp December afternoon. A few yards away, another group gathers, and another. Soon, there are more people in the forest than there are trees. Then, above the feverish buzz of excitement, comes a shout.

"Here it comes!" As one, the patient onlookers stop their talking and strain to hear a faint noise in the distance.

They peer up the track into the thick tree-lined distance, watching and waiting.

An intermittent low-pitched sound echoes through the mist. The noise grows from a rumble into a growl; then suddenly there is an explosion of noise — a crash, a bang, a high-pitched mechanical scream. Stones and mud spray the group as they clap and cheer wildly, and the flying object hurls itself past and on into the distance. Those fortunate few spectators were watching history in the making — a British driver on his way to winning the RAC Rally.

Early December in 1972 is a time to treasure for any rally enthusiast. But for those who were there and watching, the memory is priceless.

Even as youngsters start their rallying careers today, one man will probably have provided them with their inspiration, and the spectators in Grizedale Forest were witness to the closing moments of this man's finest performance.

And the man? Roger Albert Clark.

To this day, and despite all that has been made of the coincidence over the years, Roger Clark still smiles to himself as he reflects on his initials.

Like every RAC Rally before and since, speculation on the 1972 event centred upon the keenest hope of every British rally enthusiast. This time, perhaps, one of our home crews could at last win our own event.

Starting at number four, Roger carried the dreams of a nation. But not everyone was convinced the man from Leicestershire could do it. His own team manager was sceptical, and said so. Indeed, for Ford's Stuart Turner, only the Finns and the Swedes had the necessary skills and qualities to win world championship events.

"There was an invasion of Scandinavians, and I was the only Englishman doing my bit," Roger recalls. "I did get a lot of flak and, yes, Turner was very pro-Scandinavian at the time, and obviously the Scandinavians were doing very well. I knew I could compete with them quite happily, but as always on the RAC you've got to have a run where no problems occur. The '72 RAC was one of those rallies where things went right from the word go — that's the way you win such events."

Roger started cautiously; there was too much at stake to be thrown away by an early mistake. "We were just bedding ourselves in," he says. He was partnered by Tony Mason, an able and experienced co-driver, who subsequently went on to help manage the Ford team, before becoming a television presenter.

An early charge from Hakan Lindberg in his Lancia 124 ended with a broken axle. From then on, Clark and Mason took the lead and held it, despite the efforts of Stig Blomqvist in his Saab 96 V4.

"Stig was giving us a lot of heartache," Clark remembers. Nevertheless, by the halfway halt at York Racecourse, he had a precious minute and a half cushion over the flying Swede.

Clark admits to two advantages he held over his Swedish rival.

Firstly, he had just won the RAC British Championship, and had been thrashing around the British forests (many used again on the RAC) all year. Secondly, he had the latest engine, with a brand new fuel injection system. The Escort had moved on from the old cast-iron 1800cc unit to the new alloy two-litre version earlier in the year,. But for the RAC, the carburettors were swapped in favour of the Lucas injection system. "It gave us hardly any more top-end power, but a lot more torque," Roger claims. "In the forests, of course, especially the dirty, slippery, horrible forests of that year's RAC, that was good."

He was also extremely familiar with the car. The Ford team was made up entirely of Scandinavian drivers apart from Roger, so he carried out all the test and development work on the works Escort, as it made more financial sense for Stuart Turner to use a home-based man instead of going to the expense of flying in someone like Hannu Mikkola all the time. Clark denies this gave him any further advantage, though: "I think the main things we were doing at the time were just to get the car more reliable."

Dirty, slippery and horrible the 1972 RAC Rally was indeed. "I remember in the northern forests, especially on the west side in Cumbria and Scotland, it was damp and windy, with puddles everywhere. The inside of the car was wet, everything was getting steamed up every time you got a bit sweaty. It was one of those events which wasn't very pretty. I remember it being quite foggy and misty at nights as well."

The RAC in 1972 was very much different from the short sharp event it is today. It may still run over four or five days, but now it has long overnight rest halts, and much shorter stages. In '72, it was a case of flat-out driving for two days and a night, a brief halt, and then another two days without rest. Roger, familiar with the rally's demands, had planned his strategy carefully. "I've always spent the first half of a long event like that settling myself in and doing my own thing, and then planned the second half for an attack if necessary," he explains.

By the second half of the rally, people were beginning to get excited. Clark was holding Blomqvist at bay, and was pacing himself for the finish. It looked like a British driver would beat the Scandinavians, and perhaps Stuart Turner would have to eat his words. Roger Clark was headline news:

"There were reports every day in the daily newspapers — which you don't get any more. I think the publicity and general public awareness was more then than it is even now," he claims.

All eyes were on Clark, but the pressure never really bothered him. "It was my challenge," he says, "and only I could do it. It was nice having a lot of fans behind me, but the way I looked at it was that I had a job to do and I just had to get on with it. The hardest thing was to strike a balance between going berserk and simply staying in front.

"It was certainly hard work, though. I think the second night was hardest of all. I always felt worst during the RAC at the time when you'd normally be going to bed in the evening — about eleven o'clock — and you knew you had another six hours of slogging through the mud and darkness ahead. But the only time you really get down is when something goes wrong. Then the adrenalin stops, and you feel wet and cold..."

Nothing did go wrong, however. Not on the stages anyway. It was after all the stages were finished that Clark had his first and only major setback, and it was enough almost to snatch victory away from him. The most memorable achievement in British rallying history was nearly lost on the final 100-mile road section back to York.

Clark and Mason were calmly making their way back from the Lake District, basking in the glorious thought that they were about to become the first Brits to win the modern-day RAC. Then came a horrible screeching sound. Clark's heart sank, as he realised a wheel bearing had broken. Could this be possible? After nearly 70 tough stages without a problem, was the car going to let him down now?

"It really was a bit of panic," he laughs. "It just seized up and broke. All we had to do was drive the last few miles and clock in at the last control. Everyone was driving back across the moors for the finish, so there was a lot of help around. But to strip a whole wheel assembly off and re-fit the hub was 10 or 15 minutes, and we only had 20 minutes to spare. It was all a bit fraught. It nearly spoilt the rally!"

Luckily, Andrew Cowan, who had dropped out of the event in his Escort in Scotland, had been chasing Clark around in case he was needed to help out. If it wasn't for the Scotsman, all might have been lost. Andrew was on the scene like a shot, and soon LVX 942J, that famous Team Esso Uniflo Escort, was safely on its way to champagne and glory. When it finally arrived, the new British heroes were lost in a horde of reporters, photographers, and TV cameras.

"It was tremendous. The RAC's the best event in the world. It was a great level-tester for everyone, so that was the one to win. It put us on the next level."

And what did Stuart Turner say afterwards? "He, er… didn't say anything!" Roger laughs, "I think we'd proved our point by then! It was a turning point. It was the first milestone on the way to the big time, I suppose."

Clark and Mason became instant celebrities after the RAC win and were soon accustomed to the attentions of the media.

Winning the RAC brought accolades. Here, Clark receives the Segrave Trophy, accompanied by (left to right) Mick Jones, Team Manager Peter Ashcroft, Stuart Turner and Tony Mason.

LOCAL HERO

It's difficult to imagine Clark as no more than a "clubman" motor sports enthusiast. But like thousands of other young hopefuls before and since, he too had to start at the very bottom and suffer the setbacks, brush-offs and disappointments that form almost every driver's apprenticeship. It can safely be said, in fact, that Clark suffered more than most and that if it hadn't been for his extraordinary determination and self-belief, he would never have reached the top — the very top — as Britain's most famous rally driver.

Even after many years of retirement, Clark remains a legend in the rallying world, enjoying a place among a handful of British sporting heroes whose achievements have transcended generations.

The starting-point for Clark was relatively humble. His family was by no means poor, but it wasn't rich, either. Nor did he have a rallying heritage to call upon. More than that, rallying as we know it today had not really been invented when Roger first took to the roads. His progress from a being a young man having a laugh with his mates to becoming a rallying legend vividly confirms the old saying that "talent will out".

Roger was born in August 1939, in Narborough, Leicestershire, where his father owned a private local bus service. Soon after the outbreak of war, the entire fleet of buses was commandeered by the RAF, and the family business turned its attention to a machine shop making gun barrels. When hostilities ended, Mr Clark was offered his vehicles back, but after several years' hard active service they were in no fit state to provide their owner with a livelihood. With characteristic enterprise, the machine shop was converted to a workshop with a forecourt and a car repair business was established. By the time Roger was completing his schooling, there were, as he recalls, "two or three mechanics and my Dad, and that was it".

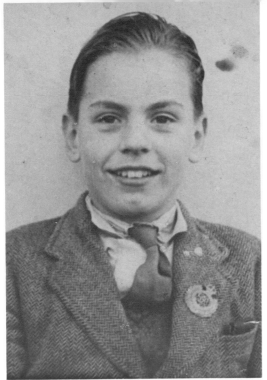

Left: Roger the schoolboy. In 1949, when this picture was taken, who would have known that this young tearaway was going to become the most famous British rally driver ever?

Below: One of Clark's major loves outside rallying is rugby. In this photo of the Hinckley Grammar School team, he is third player from right in the back row.

Bottom: Autocrossing the Renault Dauphine was just one of Clark's early motorsport experiences.

The lifelong love-affair with cars was about to begin in earnest for young Clark. It started, like many love-affairs, one late summer's day.

After a long and lazy summer holiday, reflecting on good exam results and the promise of further academic success, Roger set out for the bus-stop on his way to begin a new scholastic year. He stood there waiting for the bus to arrive, thinking about the future; and then, just as the bus was pulling up, there occurred one of those pivotal moments which change the course of a life.

"I just didn't get on," Clark remembers. "It was that close. I went back to Dad and asked him for a job."

From then on, cars became the paramount concern in his life. Motor sport came later and almost by chance when, "as a sort of public relations exercise," he went along to his local motor club. A few of his customers belonged to the Leicester Car Club and had urged Roger to attend one of its meetings as it could be good for business. The bug bit, and before too long he was racing, rallying, autotesting and autocrossing everything and anything he could lay hands on, virtually every weekend.

Transport in those early days was whatever was available, even if it was more cart-horse than thoroughbred material. While few young hopefuls in the nineties would think of setting a wheel near a race-track without the latest set-up, back in the late fifties Clark would borrow a Ford 100E van and make up in enthusiasm what he lacked in equipment.

"The Car Club was very strong; I got into a friendly crowd who were all into the same things, and it was good sport. Their enthusiasm was contagious and I simply joined in. But it really was make-do-and-mend in those days. We couldn't afford new cars, or anything of that sort."

It was at Leicester Car Club that Roger met someone who was to have an important influence on his rallying career. The year was 1960, and the man, who was to be his co-driver on many memorable rallies, was Jim Porter.

"He was co-driving for someone else then," Clark remembers. "But for one reason and another I was doing more events, and Jim started co-driving and navigating for me instead. Eventually he was with me all the time."

Road rallying was all the rage in those days. Modern stage rallying was all-but unknown, and with uncongested roads, few roadworks and even fewer traffic jams, it was relatively easy for clubs to run competitive rallies on open public roads during the night, and through country lanes. Roger didn't have too much success, to begin with. After a succession of poor navigators and disappointing runs, he was growing somewhat disenchanted with rallying and forming a preference for racing and autotesting where he had to depend on no-one but himself. His attitude changed when Porter came along, but the cars were still basic.

"After starting with the garage van, we went on to an 850 Mini when they came on to the second-hand market. Then we took on a Renault agency, and when the Dauphine arrived I nicked the garage demonstrator to go rallying."

It was a sign of things to come. Despite not having the money to buy or build competition cars, he did have the advantage of selling second-hand and new cars from the family garage. At first the van was pressed into service, when no-one else was using it at the weekends; and then, growing bolder, he progressed to demonstrators. Roll cages, fire extinguishers, racing harnesses and all the other modern paraphernalia were not needed back in 1960. Clark simply took the demonstrator (whatever was quickest at the time), slapped on a sumpguard and a few extra lights, then cleaned it up and reinstated it in the showroom on Monday morning.

It was in 1961 in the Dauphine Gordini demonstrator that Clark, with Jim Porter, won his first rally. The Sturgess Trophy was a small, closed-to-club event, and despite making him something of a local hero, victory was hardly earth-shattering. It was, however, a much-needed confidence-booster — and, fresh from his Sturgess success he set off to enter, of all things, an international rally!

The Circuit of Ireland Rally, held over the Easter weekend, was far from the high-speed thrash around Ireland it was later to

Above: Home-built cars were the order of the day in 1960. This car was made up of two halves, the front red, the rear white. — Below: Preparation was minimal. This Mini demonstrator from the Clark garage was one of Roger's first rally cars.

become. Closing the roads to the public to run special stages was simply unheard of then: it was more of a gentlemanly tour, with lots of navigational exercises and a few driving tests, or autotests as they're now called, thrown in for good measure.

The Dauphine was hardly the most suitable of cars. As Roger admits: "We didn't stand a chance. The Dauphine's handling wasn't the best, to put it mildly, and the driving tests were being won by Minis and Sprites. Local knowledge on the navigational sections played a big part, too, so a young foreigner with a strange co-driver in a Dauphine certainly couldn't raise his hopes too high!"

Fifty-first overall was hardly a sign of things to come. But Clark valued the adventure: "It was good experience for us, which was what we wanted."

His early career was linked inexorably to the family business. When he was selling Renaults, he had to drive Renaults. But as luck would have it, later in 1961 the family business acquired a BMC agency. This was crucial to Clark. At last he could get his hands on a Mini Cooper, currently the best rally car around.

"Yep, I nicked the demonstrator right away!" he recalls with a chuckle.

Fortunately, there was little opposition to Roger's unorthodox weekend use of the demonstrators. He explains: "I started the sales department anyway. Father didn't do any selling. He wasn't very interested in the rallying, but I was lucky because he didn't disapprove of it either. It was only when I became a bit more successful that he began taking an interest." It must have been quite an experience buying a car from Clark's of Narborough at that time, with this young competitor taking customers on demonstration runs in cars which had probably already finished a few rallies!

The Cooper didn't arrive until 1962, so at first Roger had to make do with a standard 850. It was in this car that he made his RAC Rally debut.

"It was a bog-standard Mini, and three up!" he exclaims. In those very different days, three people in a car was still permitted.

Special Stages, however, had been invented by this time. A European concept, they were introduced into the forests that year by Clerk of the Course, Jack Kelmsley. Kelmsley had taken over the running of the RAC in 1959, and made it into the rally it is today.

These forestry special stages were new to everyone, especially young Clark. But faced with two thousand miles or more of competitive motoring, and with little chance of sleep, he thought a third person in the car might help.

It was quite an experience, though a mistake to take a third man. "It was a very long event, and what with rough roads and the Mini with three-up, we didn't do much good to the suspension." The real importance of the rally was that it finally set Clark on the course he wanted to take, towards the success he was determined to find. Although he had always been very enthusiastic about motor sport in general, this inauspicious RAC debut focused his ambitions purely on rally driving — though a placing of 52nd overall could hardly have given the future double-RAC winner grounds for optimism.

The following year, armed with a Mini Cooper, Clark was to start making a name for himself, especially at home. He completed only four major events, but took part in a host of local rallies. With the new car, he was no longer at any sort of disadvantage and there were signs of a genuine talent beginning to emerge.

Yet again, for financial reasons the Cooper was minimally equipped. At first, it had just a sumpguard and rear lights, but later it was transformed. "I forget what I did to it exactly," Clark confesses, "but after a while I had it turned into a proper rally car".

For 1962, Clark had decided to contest the East Midlands Championship. The Eastwood Rally was his first event in the new car, and he promptly won it.

Marking his first "restricted" win, one step up from local club events, this was a significant milestone. Restricted rallies formed, and still do form, the bulk of area championship rallies. A second

Opposite: It wasn't long before Roger, pictured here with brother Stan, started amassing trophies.

place on his next rally a few weeks later was soon followed by wins on the Dukeries and Rolls-Royce Motor Club rallies. By the end of the season, he was East Midlands Champion.

Though naturally elated at taking the title, Clark still nurtured international ambitions. In the same year, along with all the local rallies he could enter, he competed in the Circuit of Ireland, Scottish, Gulf London and RAC rallies. The first of these was a totally different story from that of the previous year: in the Mini Cooper, Clark managed to win his class and finish fourth overall. The Scottish, though a disappointment in terms of its result, was still another valuable confidence-builder. Partnered by Roger Marriott (Jim Porter had examinations to sit and couldn't come), Clark was sitting comfortably in second place overall behind Andrew Cowan when they got badly lost. The consequent loss of time saw them finishing firmly at the bottom, but up until the mistake there had been an inkling of what was to come. The Scottish, like the RAC, included special stages and Clark had already found these much to his liking. By then, he was developing his unique style for driving on gravel forest roads — a little too sideways for most people's taste!

All this rallying inevitably required a degree of funding, which Clark still couldn't easily afford. 1962, however, witnessed his first-ever sponsorship deal. By then, his local reputation and his achievements in the East Midlands Championship were making him known to a widening circle of enthusiasts, among them a business associated with the family garage.

"The Capital Finance Company… " Clark ponders a moment. "Yes, I remember twisting two hundred pounds out of them, somehow."

Once again, running a car dealership had proved to have certain advantages!

LIA ESTATE CAR
The
ReMARKABl
DATE with the DAUPHINE
performance...
...quality
XJU 2

Above: Those early Minis took a battering!
Below: Like many other drivers of the era, Clark cut his teeth on night-time road rallies. This picture was taken on the 1963 Cat's Eye Rally.

the Alps at seven thousand feet, I can tell you! But I think Rover were pleased with what we did, and we certainly put the 2000 on the map for them. I believe sixth overall and first in class on the 'sixty-five Monte Carlo was our best result, which was quite good for that car. That was fantastic, that drive. I mean, a car that heavy up the Alps… to get up to sixth overall was no small thing. It was very snowy and slippery, but we had good studs and a really good run. Rover were delighted: I'm sure they'd never expected to do that well."

The Monte Carlo Rally also provided Clark with his first experience of making pace notes. And, while he found this new trick to be advantageous, he also developed an aversion to it over the years. As he explains:

"I don't like making them at all, to be honest. Practising is just boring; you get fed up with yourself, and that just gets you bad-tempered. So, no, I don't enjoy pace noting, though I have to admit I like using them. Once you've done them and used them properly, the satisfaction justifies the effort."

Meanwhile, life in the British Championship was improving with a momentum he could scarcely have predicted back when he started in 1961. Thanks in large part to Henry Taylor, it was now all coming together very nicely indeed.

Since the '64 Scottish win, Taylor had regarded Clark as a protégé, with a talent to be nurtured. "Henry and I struck it off from the word go. He started giving me parts for my car, found me small jobs to do, and slowly wound me into the team. He took a big interest, gave me just the kind of encouragement a young driver needs."

After a string of retirements, culminating with the Welsh Rally in January 1965, Clark's white Cortina GT began simply to fall apart. Taylor stepped into the breach with a new body shell. This "new" bright red car was to take Clark to third on the Circuit of Ireland Rally that year, followed by victories on the Scottish, the Gulf London, and the December Welsh Rally. It was enough to give him the crown he was to wear many times over the years: that of British RAC Rally Champion.

Above: On his last drive for Rover, Clark took fourteenth overall on the 1965 RAC Rally.
Below: In 1964 Clark scored his first international win on the Scottish Rally in his privately run
Cortina GT. Works cars were out of contention and Ford support service crews moved in to help.

"Once you get a factory behind you like that, life begins to open up for you and get different ideas. It was all changing."

It was a heroic effort by Clark. He also had a full works programme with Rover, remember. And in June, he attempted two major rallies in one month — the Scottish and the Gulf London — and won them both.

"It was a time when I was getting quite cocky and confident," Clark says candidly. "They were two good events for the car. We were getting all the parts from Ford, and Dunlop gave me some tyres. Basically, we were scrounging whatever we could. I mean, I used to fettle all the cars myself, with all the spares from Ford.

"It wasn't so expensive then. The cars were far closer to standard, and didn't have a lot of high-price kits on like they do now. Back then, it was a case of wreck it Saturday and fix it Monday."

It was a busy time. But then, despite his often laid-back public image, there was rarely a time when Clark wasn't busy. Nor is there ever likely to be.

"It wasn't a chore to me then," he insists. "Messing around with motor cars was my life and I enjoyed it. Work wasn't such hard work as it is today!"

The year also brought him closer to a full-time position within the Ford team. The 1965 Tulip Rally in April was his first works drive for Ford and "it was virtually all works drives from then on".

There were difficulties too, though. Clark had developed a strong sense of loyalty to Ralph Nash and the Rover team, and there was Jim Porter to consider. Since Jim and Roger had moved to the team together, Jim had given up his planned career in the meat industry to take up a position with Rover, helping with the administration of the competition department and interspersing his office duties with co-driving for Roger. It was a convenient arrangement, but eventually, when Rover's competition department closed, it left Porter stranded. But Roger had little choice but to move. Given his career situation and the strength of Ford's rallying commitment at that time, it would have been madness not to.

"It wasn't too much of a wrench, really. The Ford team was obviously a lot more competitive, so it was a move right up the ladder and quite a big deal for me. It was just Ford and BMC, in those days. They were the two big teams to be with."

By this time, Henry Taylor had moved into management at Ford and Clark slotted in alongside such drivers as Vic Elford, Bengt Soderstrom, and David Seigle-Morris. At last he had the drive he wanted and the larger recognition his hard-won skills had earned. From those humble beginnings, begging and borrowing from the family workshop, thrashing around fields and lanes in club events, he was finally in with one of the biggest names in the business. It was a relationship destined to last many years, bringing major success, a measure of conflict, and a fame almost unrivalled in rallying history.

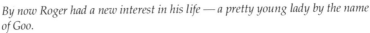

By now Roger had a new interest in his life — a pretty young lady by the name of Goo.

THE BIG TIME

The Welsh International in December 1965 was the starting point of Clark's full-time career with Ford. He celebrated in style, finishing first and clinching the British Championship, this time in a Lotus Cortina. The new car handled just the same way his old GT did, which he liked, but was significantly more powerful.

"It was much better," he maintains. "My old car was virtually standard, but this new works car was the proper job." And not surprisingly, after the long and sometimes lonely years of having to fend for himself: "To be paid for rallying, and have mechanics chasing you around and looking after you, was really super."

His British Championship crown was the first of five, a record he was to hold until Jimmy McRae equalled it in 1987 and overtook it a year later. Enthusiasts in those days rarely bothered to ask of a rally, "Who won?" It was more realistic to phrase the question, "By how much did Roger win this time?"

But that was still all ahead of him. At the start of 1966, Clark's immediate and over-riding concern was a full works programme with Ford, starting with the Monte Carlo Rally. Readers even vaguely interested in rallying will recall that year's Monte as one of the great absurdities in the sport's history. For Clark and others, it certainly didn't provide the season with the smoothest of starts. 1966 was the year of the infamous illegal lights controversy, when virtually everyone bar the French was thrown out, allegedly so that a Citroen could win a home event. The details have been covered many times before, but suffice to say it caused an outrage in Britain and did absolutely nothing at all for *l'entente cordiale*. The winning three Minis (headed by Paddy Hopkirk) were all disqualified, along with Roger's Escort, for having non-standard light bulbs. Roger had been fourth before the disqualification, but the resulting furore in England more than made up for it. As Clark recalls:

"It was just stupid, really, but I think we got as much publicity

out of it as if we'd come in first! It certainly didn't do us any harm; in fact, with anti-French feelings running as high as they did, we seemed to have the whole world on our side."

Prior to the disqualifications, Clark's driving had earned him a moral victory. In snowy conditions, far better suited to the Minis than his rear-wheel-drive Lotus Cortina, he had been the best of the rest and had attracted considerable recognition and press coverage.

The biggest event of the year was his wedding. Clark still breaks into a broad grin when describing the day, and indeed the honeymoon, which neither he nor his wife Judith are likely ever to forget. He had met Judith — or Goo, as she is universally known — at the Leicester Motor Club driving test, and it wasn't long before Goo was having some serious lessons in what it meant to be married to a works rally driver. Even the ceremony itself was different, with Henry Taylor sending along three of the works Fords to be used as wedding cars. It was the honeymoon, though, that really took the biscuit.

"We got married and flew straight out to Athens," Clark says, "and then the next morning I went out to do the recce for the Acropolis. So she had quite a lonely honeymoon I'm afraid!"

In fairness to Roger, it has to be said he hadn't planned it that way. Brian Melia, his co-driver for the event, had flown out in advance of the newly-weds to compile the pace notes for the rally, but had hurt his back and couldn't continue. Consequently, Roger had to leave Brian at the hotel to keep Goo company, while he finished the task himself. Not the most romantic honeymoon in the world, in other words! But in rallying terms the trip to Greece was successful, with Clarke and Melia achieving a creditable second place.

All in all, it was a season of mixed fortunes, the Acropolis and another second place on the Coupe des Alpes being Clark's best results. Clark also learned the full meaning of being a works driver when Ford packed him off to compete in an unusual event in Canada, which he didn't like at all. "It was a totally different sort of rallying, with very little in the way of special stages," he recalls of the Shell 4000 Rally. "We just went down the main road and nipped off into the forests every now and again. There was a lot of this regularity timing — you were hardly driving at all really, just following instructions from the co-driver. I was more like a chauffeur than a driver — I think there were only one or two stages a day." But even if he didn't enjoy the rallying, it was an interesting visit to a country he hadn't previously seen. He finished third, and was contracted to the rally again in 1967, when he took first place.

Retirement on the Circuit, Scottish, and Gulf London rallies provided the main disappointments of the year, twice with rear differential failure, but one of the year's highlights was a fourth place on the Polish Rally. Not that Roger liked the country too much, but at least it was another new experience and a successful outing for one special reason. "It was a fairly average sort of event," he claims. "but what I do remember is coming back with more money than we went out with! We could change our money on the black market for about three or four times what it was actually worth. Other than that, though, it wasn't really a place I'd recommend."

1966 was also the year when Clark, for the first and last time, tackled the 1,000 Lakes Rally. This was, and still is, an event which is very difficult for non-Scandinavian drivers. It's a fast rally, with many enormous jumps, and perfect lines are essential. As a result, local Finns who know the roads off by heart start with a massive built-in advantage.

Given the unique demands of the Lakes, and the fact that it was by no means uncommon for the top twenty or so drivers to finish only seconds apart, a placing of 19th overall was better than it sounds. But Clark certainly saw no reason for trying the rally again.

"To be in with a chance, you'd need six months living and practising over there, because the stages are of such a different character. We were just out of place there, to tell the truth. It's the sort of rally you'd have to specialise in."

The Coupe des Alpes on the other hand, in which he finished

second that year, was much more to his liking. "It's a super rally," he says. "It's a really long, hard event; very tiring, but good stages, with the classic Alpine passes."

Shortly afterwards, Clark had a very special surprise. He knew he was down to drive on the Lombard RAC Rally, but what he didn't know was that his namesake, the legendary Grand Prix racing driver Jim Clark, was also entered for the event and that Roger had been entrusted with teaching him how to drive a rally car! So off he went to Bagshot to introduce one of the nation's racing heroes to the demands of driving in the forests. It was an experience Roger was never to forget, and the great Scotsman impressed him deeply.

"Jim was an absolute natural," he reveals. "A genius, really, just like everyone says. He simply sat in and watched me for a few minutes, then got behind the wheel and did the business. He learned very quickly. It was a great honour, and we got on exceptionally well together. It was also a fantastic contrast, because I did the same thing with Graham Hill and he was like a fish out of water in the rally car — couldn't get the hang of it, try as he might."

Unfortunately, neither of the Clarks fared too well on the rally. Jim, having set fastest time on three stages and been at one time in sixth place, retired from the fray after a couple of pretty enormous accidents, while Roger's Lotus Cortina had a new type of limited slip differential, imported from America, which didn't suit him at all. It tended to grip too suddenly, pushing the nose of the car off the road, and Roger ended the rally with an accident while leading.

"It was bloody dangerous," he admits. "I can tell you, that diff was removed from the specification *tout de suite!*"

Predictably, Ford were reluctant to take part in the 1967 Monte Carlo Rally; in fact, the previous year's debacle prompted a total refusal to enter. Ford of Germany, however, were keen to contest the event, and the importer wanted Roger to drive. The car, a Taunus 20M, was a big, lumbering machine, desperately unsuited to rallying, but Clark took up the challenge.

Above: Wedding bells! Roger and Goo were soon on their way to Greece for a honeymoon... and a spot of rallying!
The wedding "limo", courtesy of Ford, was Clark's own works car.
Below: Clark and Brian Melia set off on the 1966 Monte Carlo Rally.

Above: After a superb drive on the Monte Carlo, Clark was disqualified along with three winning Minis due to the famous lights controversy. He would have been fourth, but had won a moral victory and gained major publicity. — Below: With a works team like Ford, one expects a few adventures. This one was in Poland.

Above: Racing played a small part in the Ford programme and our man Clark was given a Cortina to play with on the circuits. — Below: He doesn't look too happy. After the '66 disqualification, Ford refused to send a works team to the Monte Carlo. Ford of Germany entered Roger in a Taunus, a tank of a machine which he didn't enjoy.

Above: In 1967 the Lotus Cortina fell apart on the Safari, but didn't dampen Clarke's love of the rally.

Below: On his way to winning one of the first "proper" rallies in the Mk 2 Lotus Cortina — the 1967 Scottish.

"It was a 2.3 litre V6 tank!" he exclaims. "Big, heavy, slow — the equivalent, you could say, of our own Ford Zephyr." An inauspicious 67th was all Clark could manage, after being demoted from 22nd on scratch times after the Group 2 handicap was applied. (And no, he can no more explain the ruling now than most people could then, confining himself to the simple comment that "it was all a bit of a joke".)

Clark also took to the race tracks that year. Having competed in a few races in his formative club days, he decided he would like to try again, this time "in an old recce car that Henry (Taylor) lent me — a bit of an old nail, really." The idea behind the decision was to gain experience on tarmac, and to learn all the race tracks.

One race in particular stands out in his mind: "It was at Mallory Park; we had only one set of racing tyres and it was peeing down with rain, so I asked the scrutineers if I could fit the car with a set of forest tyres. And they said, 'if you're daft enough, go ahead,' so I did and we won the race quite easily, with plenty of sideways!" In fact, his racing performances were sufficiently encouraging for Calypso, the cigarette company, to back him the following year in a Cortina, when "we didn't win a lot, but we had a lot of fun trying."

Had he gone more seriously into racing, as he easily could have done, we might well have seen Roger Clark the Grand Prix driver, instead of Clark the rallying great. But he turned the opportunity down flat. For a start, the elements of racing which he really enjoyed were too few and far between to mount a serious challenge to his rallying career: "You spend a lot of time hanging around doing nothing, in order to put in a very limited amount of actual competitive driving." And then there was another event, its impact altogether starker and more immediate. "When Jimmy (Clark) was killed, Ford said to me, 'Do you want to take his place?' I just said: 'If that's what it did for him, I don't want to follow.'

"It isn't just that rallying's more interesting to me," Clark expounds; "it's more of a challenge as well. I find the racing good fun, but every race is the same. So even though I'd certainly recommend it to any driver as a valuable learning experience, the lesson I learned from it myself was that it wasn't for me."

As is borne out by results, it was a relatively lean year for Clark. But at least he managed to finish the East African Safari, even though his car was falling apart. That was his last event in the Mk 1 Lotus Cortina. Shortly afterwards, he appeared in the new Mk 2 shell which, due to its inherent structural weaknesses, was never going to make a great rally car. But Roger wasn't unduly worried. He knew what was coming next: the announcement of a new car from Ford which was to achieve a truly remarkable record in rallying and with which his name was to be permanently and inextricably linked.

Dig those groovy jackets, man! Clark with Ove Andersson in 1968, after receiving their award for leading the London-Sydney Marathon halfway through.

Above: The Escort arrives! Clark took part in the early development of the Ford Escort. Here he is pictured suspension testing.
Left: Stuart Turner gave Clark grounds for anxiety when he arrived at Ford as the boss. Turner made no secret of his preference for Scandinavian drivers.

ESCORT GLORY

It was a big secret at the time. During 1967, while it appeared that Clark was having an unprecedently quiet year, he was hard at work testing Ford's new rally weapon — the Escort Twin-Cam.

From his first encounter with the twin-cam, Clark was convinced that it was the rally car of the future.

Roger Clark is famous mainly for being the only British driver to win the modern RAC Rally. But he also holds a place in enthusiasts' hearts as the first man to rally the Escort — still the mainstay of rallying today, albeit at club level only. It was a special and, at the time, revolutionary machine. Not that it was technically advanced; but in terms of design, construction and handling, it was practically the perfect rally car.

"We were very excited about it," he recalls. "And the next year when it came out, we won just about everything we entered."

In 1968, after retiring on the Swedish rally due to illness (a stomach bug) in the Cortina, Clark wheeled out the new Escort for its debut on the Circuit of Ireland Rally and promptly took first place.

He had also been involved in the testing of the GT70, which was supposed to be Ford's first rallying supercar. The low-slung sports machine, which at the time bore more resemblance to a spaceship than a car, never made the grade.

"It was a dog. And it never had the chance to get sorted out, to be honest. But they tried to make it out of all Ford standard parts, which was a mistake. You can't make a competition car from standard parts out of a bin. I think Ford wanted to get into the European rallies, where Renault were doing very well with the A110 Alpine. The GT70 was designed for the Alps and French tarmac rallying, but it never worked."

Thanks in part to the oil crisis, the GT70 project was cut out completely at the end of 1973.

The Escort, though, was a different proposition altogether. "It was absolutely fabulous. It was the perfect size and shape. The engine by that time had been sorted out in the Lotus Cortina, so immediately, it was a very good car. It was more nimble than the Cortina, and handled better. Suddenly we were in a different league with the Escort. It was a big step ahead for us, and everything about the car suited my personal style."

Clark's first big international win in the car came in the 1968 Tulip Rally. A number of variations on the Escort theme quickly followed. The first attempt at improving the power output came just before the Coupe des Alpes, when Clark completed the recce with a Formula 2 FVA 16-valve engine. It was replaced by the old Lotus twin-cam for the event, however, since the racing engine was found to be totally unsuitable for rallying. The size was increased to from 1600cc to 1800cc by April 1969, and by early 1970 the first of the famous Cosworth BDA 16-valve engines had been fitted.

In the meantime, Clark wasn't quite finished with the Lotus Cortina. In November 1968, he was entered with Ove Andersson in one of the all-time great motorsport events: the London-Sydney Marathon. This was a massive media extravaganza, which captured the imagination of enthusiasts throughout the world. The scale of the Marathon is hard to imagine today, with only the Paris-Dakar in any way resembling its format. The competitors would make a long, high-speed trek from London, through Europe, across the Middle East to Asia, before heading down through India to Bombay. From there, the crews, cars and back-up were to be shipped across to Australia, where the final section would take them from the North of the continent, South through the outback, to Sydney.

Clark led almost from the start — all the way across Europe, through the Middle East and Asia. At Bombay, as they boarded the ship to Australia after seven days of constant, hard driving, he looked virtually un-catchable. Most of the way across Australia, too, he led. And then, with victory all but within his grasp, it happened...

"The rally would finish about nine or ten o'clock that morning, and we had problems about five o'clock. The crown wheel to the diff unit came loose. As luck would have it, we stopped another Cortina on the road, did a deal, stripped the two cars down on the side of the road, changed the diff, and I finished tenth."

It was a bitter pill, breaking down so close to the finish, but Clark takes pride in having completed the Marathon. While many other teams had a third crew member in each car, he had elected to have only a single co-driver. For the London-Sydney, the co-driver was exactly that — they shared the driving. That was why he chose Andersson, who was also a top-name driver at the time.

It's a measure of Clark's committment that he decided to do things this way. He was never one for the easier option, and hard work in the driving or co-driving seat of a rally car was hardly likely to worry him. Furthermore, it was only by a cruel stroke of ill-luck that his determination and foresight failed to bring him — and Andersson too, of course — the prize they deserved.

On the next big marathon event, the 16,000 mile London-Mexico World Cup, which involved an enormous circuit of South America, Clark put his foot down again. Other teams went to recce the continent and came back highly concerned at the prospect: three drivers in a tank was the only way they would consider participating. But having taken a look himself, Clark assured the team that two drivers in each car were more than enough and that, in his opinion, an Escort was exactly the right car for the job.

Ford took his advice and, while it paid off for the team, for Clark himself the result wasn't too happy.

"I've always said the best thing for any marathon event is a strong and simple car," he maintains. "And that's what we decided to go for with the Escort. That was one hell of a long event!" The body was, in Clark's words, "made into one big roll cage," but it still wasn't strong enough for co-driver, Alec Poole. Clark describes the incident:

"I was leaning backwards on my seat getting some food out of the back for him, and I ended up hard against the dashboard…

Above: Sideways as ever, Clark entertaining the crowds on the 1971 Welsh Rally in the Withers of Winsford Escort.

Below: Partnered by the late Henry Liddon, Clark takes a neat line on his way to winning the dry tarmac Manx Rally.

I twisted my ankle, and I think that's the only time I've ever injured myself in a car." While Clark had been fumbling around looking for food, Poole had been busy looking over his shoulder watching him. He didn't see a slow-moving Volkswagen ahead, and ploughed straight into the back of it. Nevertheless, Clark's theories on the event were validated unarguably by Hannu Mikkola, who won, and the victory gave birth to another great car, the Escort Mexico.

These were busy times for Roger, even by his own exacting standards. Not only was he involved in extensive international and national rally programmes and in looking after his burgeoning business empire, but his Ford connections had led him, professionally at least, into a totally new sport — powerboat racing. Clark has been seriously interested in power boats for almost as long as he can remember and is involved with them even today, importing boats through his company, Roger Clark Marine. It was in 1969 that Ford asked him to drive a boat fitted with one of their new marine diesel engines, and Clark describes the experience with enthusiasm:

"For many years we did class three racing, which is twenty-five-foot boats and three outboard engines. I'd actually been powerboat racing in my own right for years before the Ford deal. Ford were bringing out a new range of diesels and wanted to promote this fact. So there it was: a team of powerboats for the Round Britain Race... I think we finished fourth, which wasn't at all bad, really. It was certainly quite an adventure, at any rate."

Despite all this activity, Clark had built up something of a reputation for idleness. He explains: "If you go by the record-books, you'll soon see I wasn't that idle!. But perhaps it sometimes frustrated people that I was a little bit laid-back, and didn't get excited too easily. Jim was very quiet, too, and people can easily draw the wrong conclusions from that."

1970 was Clark's final season in full international rallying for a number of years. It started well: a fifth on the Smile Rally in Finland with TV presenter Clement Freud, followed by another fifth on the Monte Carlo with Jim Porter. Clark debuted the new

Cosworth BDA on the Circuit and won that event yet again; but from that point on, it was just one disaster after another. He got lost with a local navigator on the Jamaica 1000, retired from the Scottish and TAP rallies with engine failure, and went out on the RAC with a broken half-shaft. There has hardly been a sportsman in the world, in any era, who hasn't suffered at one time or another from a run of ill-luck, and Clark was no exception.

The new decade had also ushered in some developments at Ford, and for Clark it was a slightly worrying time. A new team manager had arrived on the scene: Stuart Turner. Changes were bound to occur, and Clark couldn't be sure exactly how they would affect him. In his early days he had approached Turner for help on numerous occasions, and had been politely but firmly given the brush-off. In fact, Turner himself remembers the very first occasion he came across Clark, when Roger's father approached him at a rally forum:

"A bloke just turned up and said, 'My son's a talented driver'," he recalls. "Of course, there were a lot of blokes with talented sons in those days! I remember mumbling something like 'I'm sure he is,' and making my excuses. I didn't know then, of course, that I'd wind up changing jobs to find myself working with Roger Clark!"

Turner's BMC years had left him flushed with success and, worst of all for Clark, convinced that no-one but Scandinavian drivers could drive rally cars fast enough to win major international rallies. Needless to say, Clark wasn't then, and isn't now, remotely Scandinavian!

"I was apprehensive," Roger admits. "Father had spoken to him when I was driving a Mini, and he'd basically said go away and play! So obviously when he came to Ford, I was a little bit suspicious. He was on a big high with Finnish drivers and thought that no British driver was any good. We were due for a very lean year…"

Turner, while agreeing that at the time he thought Scandinavians a better bet, says now that Clark had no reason to worry. "Dropping Roger was never in my mind," he states firmly. "I remember the year the Minis were thrown out of the Monte Carlo,

Above: "Now, how many fingers am I holding up?" Clark gets the countdown at the start of a competitive section on the London-Mexico World Cup Rally. — Below: The damage doesn't look too bad, but co-driver Alec Poole's shunt into the rear of a VW put Clark out of the World Cup Rally. Team-mate Hannu Mikkola won the event.

Above: Roger at full chat in the Escort on gravel, conditions in which he revelled. This 1972 picture shows him in the famous Esso car. — Below: This famous photograph of Clark was taken on the 1972 Dukeries Rally. He won the event, and went on that year to win both the National Championship and, of course, the RAC Rally.

and Roger was fourth, which proved to me he was competent. He had a good name and was well-known in Britain. Even though I introduced Scandinavians to Ford, I fully intended to keep Roger on."

The development of the GT70 was reaching its peak at this time, and Roger had his one and only outing in the car on the Ronde Cevenole, which ended in retirement with engine failure. The only other major international was the Safari, which also ended in retirement when the shell broke up. Otherwise, Clark recalls, "the best we could do out of Stuart was the loan of a car for British events."

Until Turner arrived, Clark had also enjoyed the personal service of just one mechanic, Norman Masters. Each driver had his own mechanic who would set up the car exactly the way he wanted it; and Norman, with whom Clark had developed a close understanding, could be counted on to wheel out a perfect "Clark car" every time. Under Turner, this system had to go. From now on, the operation was to work as a team, each car prepared identically on a production-line system — and to add insult to injury as far as Clark was concerned, each car was to be in left-hand drive form to suit the favoured Scandinavians. But as Clark explains, he and Masters soon skirted round the problem:

"There was a good deal of insider conniving involved. Norman had quite a persuasive manner in the workshop, and it just sort of happened to fit in that he had to prepare my car!" Turner was more or less aware of the situation, but although he insists that his policy was the best for the team ("It reduced the time taken to produce cars and was much more cost-effective"), he tended to turn a blind eye to it. "You can try five different methods of building cars, but at the end of the day it didn't really matter, just as long as we were winning."

At the beginning of 1971, Roger Clark was left with a much curtailed International programme, and the option of competing in the British Championship. Turner, however, wasn't much interested in helping Clark out in the British series with a full support package. The way he figured it, an Escort was bound to win one way or another, so what was the point in using Ford's resources to run one purely for Roger Clark? Roger, it appeared, was out on his own again.

It was generally believed at this time that the public had seen the last of Clark as a major force in rallying. He'd had some good years, they said, but now he had passed his peak. But Roger was more resourceful and determined than they had given him credit for. By the start of the year, he had both a car, albeit an "old nail", and a new sponsor, Esso. Against the odds, it was the beginning of another Clark era.

"The Esso deal came about purely by chance," he remembers. "I was an Esso dealer through my garage anyway, so they were the first people to approach." Esso was involved with Graham Hill at the time, but British rallying provided them with another useful promotional opportunity and, with Roger Clark at the wheel, they believed they could hardly lose.

But in "Old Gold", or "Golden Oldie" as it was sometimes called, the season wasn't too successful. A combination of working on the GT70, the two rallies abroad and a couple of retirements prevented Clark from winning the Championship. But of the events he did finish, the Granite City, Hackle, and Manx Rallies, he won all three. And he took 11th on the RAC where, in icy conditions, Scandinavian drivers occupied the top eight positions.

1972, however, was Clark's big year. From being written-off at the start of 1971, he had suddenly, and typically, turned his fortunes around. It was the year, ironically, when his career appeared to be coming to a close, that Clark made his biggest impact on the British public and won himself a place in the record books.

It started unpromisingly, with an accident on the Snowman Rally. But from then on, having dumped "Old Gold" in favour of a new car from Ford, Clark was all-but unbeatable. His worst results in '72 were two second places, one on the Scottish to Hannu Mikkola, and the other on his only foreign event of the year, the Hong Kong Rally. He won every other rally he entered bar the Lindisfarne, where a wheel fell off and he retired.

On the Jim Clark Memorial Rally in June, he was given the new alloy two-litre engine, and he was used as a guinea pig yet again on the RAC, with a new injection system.

There is no such thing, of course, as an "inevitable" winner. But given his current form, Clark's historic RAC victory was about as close as you can get. Overnight, the man who had seemed in danger of being forgotten became a national hero.

Turner was pleased. "Roger got massive coverage in Britain," he says. "1972 was one of the highlights in Ford's history."

During his early years at Ford, Roger was encouraged to take up circuit racing. At one point, it was even suggested that he take over from the late Jim Clark, with a chance of moving into Formula One. Just in case, Jackie Stewart explains the controls!

Above: Heat and dust on the Safari. Clark was leading when this photograph was taken, but retired soon after when the car's electrics burned out. — Below: Clark has won more Scottish Rallies than any other driver in British rallying history. Here he is on his way to victory in the 1973 event, with Jim Porter.

Above: The 1973 RAC Rally promised much for Clark and Mason, but they were to be disappointed. Before 1972, Roger would have been exceptionally pleased to finish second, but now it was no longer enough.
Below: Clark taking off in his efforts to catch Timo Makinen on the 1973 RAC.

Above: The RS2000 was developed for club motorsport. It was Clark's job to promote the car and he was duly entered in the 1974 Tour of Britain in the near-standard Group 1 machine. He complained of lack of power. — Below: Clark became embroiled in several hectic battles on the race tracks of the Tour of Britain with saloon car racer, Gerry Marshall.

SIMPLY THE BEST

No-one, but no-one, could touch Roger Clark. He was the British Champion, virtually a household name, and 1973 was his.

Having won the RAC, and proved that Stuart Turner was wrong about Scandinavians being better than Brits (or at any rate, than Roger Clark), one would have thought a re-instatement to lead driver on international events was in order. But apart from the Safari Rally in Africa, that was never to be. He was too valuable a commodity in the UK for one thing, and Ford had lost interest in the world scene in favour of the GT70 in European rallies.

As Turner explains: "Any motor company blows hot and cold over these options. But if we had been going full song in the World Championship, Roger would definitely have been there."

Clark's programme was busy nonetheless. There were fourteen rallies, mostly in Britain. And, apart from the RAC, he won everything he finished.

The Safari, one of Clark's favourite events (he still visits Kenya regularly), was a disappointment. He was leading by an enormous margin, over half an hour, when the exhaust manifold broke and burnt out the alternator. As he sarcastically comments:

"It was a very cleverly built car in those days — you had to take the engine out to replace the manifold! We tried. though; we actually got the engine half out and got some natives and a pole across it. But we ran out of time. We'd had a really super run until then, so it was very disappointing."

Rally after rally fell to Clark, mostly with Jim Porter, but also with Tony Mason occasionally. It was with Mason that he finished second to Makinen on the RAC Rally. After his triumph the year before, second place was something of an anti-climax. But there was good reason for it. He had been to Africa shortly before the rally, returning with a nasty bout of 'flu' which proved difficult to shake off and left him in far worse shape than the demands of the

RAC warranted. Given these circumstances, second was no mean achievement.

The 1973 Tour of Britain provided extra interest. This was a totally different style of event, combining racing with rallying. Competitors would complete road sections and stages, as with a normal rally, interspersed with races and other motorsport tests. Clark's wide-ranging motorsport experience should have made this the ideal event for him. He competed in a Capri 3-litre, with Tony Mason, but blew the electrics.

By the end of the season, the RAC Championship crown was his for the third time. It was a devastating performance, which few of his competitors will forget and which kept him constantly in the motorsport headlines.

Rallying was in severe difficulties by the time the season ended. Roger's prospects for the next year were not good at all and neither were anyone else's. The oil crisis had taken hold and most rallying programmes were cancelled pending further developments.

By May, however, the worst was over and the '74 season started up again with the Welsh, on which Roger retired soon after the start with head gasket failure. But he recovered the year with a fine win from racing driver Gerry Marshall on the Tour of Britain, this time in the new Group 1 (virtually standard class) RS2000.

On the 1974 Burmah Rally, Jim Porter made the only mistake of his career, or at least the only recorded one. Clark had started the event testing tyres, before he suddenly realised that Irishman Billy Coleman was in grave danger of winning. He immediately stepped up a gear and won the event on the stages. In all the excitement, however, Jim had either mis-read or misunderstood the regulations, and a road penalty at the final control dropped them to 41st overall.

1975 brought a return to normality (normality for Clark, that is), as he again slipped the RAC British Championship crown on his well-groomed head. It was his hair, in fact, which brought about the next great Clark era, that of the Cossack Hairspray sponsorship. If there was anyone left in Britain who still hadn't heard of him, that situation was swiftly rectified with the appearance of the first Cossack TV commercials, as Clark entered the living-rooms of virtually the entire nation.

The Cossack sponsorship came about just before the debut of the latest Mk 2 Escort, and the red Cossack big-winged Ford was soon a familiar sight on the stages. For Roger, it was in the nick of time. Esso had been backing him for two years, but after the oil crisis and Burmah Oil's demise in the face of difficult trading conditions in '74, they developed an understandable caution. Their promotional budgets were severely reduced and Roger's sponsorship deal was one of the first casualties.

"Cossack had just brought out their new hairspray, and decided a rally car driver was exactly the sort of macho image they wanted," Clark grins.

Sponsorship isn't always the easiest thing to handle for a sportsman, no matter how vital to his career, and this was especially true of Clark, whose attention to activities which don't really interest him has always been somewhat reluctant. The first part of the deal was making the television ads. Clark found these "extremely boring — but it did a lot of good for me, and I thought it was a darn good advert in the end!"

The Cossack campaign was one of the all-time classics in motorsport. It enabled Clark to keep up his hectic rallying schedule in 1975 with the new car — in which, yet again, he won the RAC Championship. The Mk 2 Escort RS1800 made its debut on the Granite City Rally in April of that year. Roger won the event, and although for the most part he found the car almost as pleasing and effective as the Mk 1, he did express a few reservations:

"I had rather mixed feelings about it at the time, because it was a heavier car. By then we had much heavier axles and the big ZF gearbox had been fitted. And although the suspension was a little bit better too, it needed the extra power to cope."

Cossack were delighted with their new protégé. On the first rally with their name on the car, the Welsh International in May, Clark won yet again. He also managed to return to foreign rallying for a time, retiring in Antibes with suspension failure, but

Above: All Clark's skill and determination wasn't enough to vanquish the Porsches on the 1974 Manx Rally. He finished third behind two of the German sports cars, but vowed to come back and beat them. — Below: Understeering his way round the 1974 RAC Rally. Clark and Mason were again disappointed, this time finishing seventh.

Above: All smiles. Clark was always happiest behind the wheel of an Escort.
Below: Clark's flamboyant driving style was always popular with spectators. 1975 was the first year of the Cossack Mk 2 Escort RS and another of Clark's RAC Rally Championship-winning years.

Above: Victory in the Mk 2 came almost as easily to Clark as in the Mk 1. Here he celebrates his 1975 Scottish win with a bottle of champagne and Jim Porter. — Below: Flying high on the tarmac Epynt stages of the 1975 Welsh Rally. Clark was equally fast whether on gravel or asphalt.

winning, with Stuart Pegg, on the South African Total Rally.

The San Remo rally was also in the programme, but turned into farce when the tyre truck didn't turn up "due to a breakdown or accident or something". They started the rally on worn practice tyres and Clark was soon obliged to bow out.

One of the year's most pleasing and satisfying rallies was the Manx International. The Mk 2 was going through an intensive development phase at that time, both to improve its performance on tarmac and in the the hope that it could compete on equal terms with the supercars of Europe such as, notably, the Porsche 911. On the Manx, Clark had the added challenge of trying to beat the Irish drivers, who flocked to the island every year and who were tarmac specialists.

"To go along and thrash them in an Escort was really quite nice," he grins. "We had a good run and I had to give it everything, but we brought it off."

You wouldn't think it from the placings, but the RAC Rally of 1975 brought bitter disappointment. Clark, with co-driver Tony Mason again, finished second to Timo Makinen, but could so easily have won.

To begin with, he had brake problems. Then to add to his difficulties, shock absorbers started breaking and even the gear-box bell-housing cracked. In all, Clark lost around seven minutes through these problems. Yet such was his tenacity that Makinen's Escort finished little more than a minute ahead. (With Tony Fowkes coming third, Escorts took 1-2-3 in the event, just as they had two years previously.)

"It was a shame," Clark says. And adds, in what is surely a masterpiece of understatement: "I remember it being a very frustrating event."

Frustration was to figure heavily through the following season. 1976 was not Clark's year — not, that is, until the RAC Rally. Bright new talents were coming on to the scene, and victories were no longer there as if for the taking.

To those used to Clark winning every UK rally in sight, it came as a shock. "What's wrong with Roger?" many would ask — as if the man were simply infallible. Yet Clark himself was enough of a realist to have been expecting it. Someday, someone would strip him of his crown. In any walk of life, that was the price you paid for reaching the top.

The young pretenders were indeed a force to be reckoned with, and one can understand with hindsight how Clark was able to see it coming. The RAC Motor Sports Association was now allowing foreign drivers to compete in the national series, and a certain new Ford signing, one Ari Vatanen, was starting to shine. Another driver, destined to become Britain's leading rallyist for a decade and a half, Russell Brookes, was beginning to hit the big time in his Andrews Heat for Hire Escort RS.

Clark was being pushed to the limit. He started well, winning the Shell Dean rally, but by the Mintex the strain was starting to show, as he rolled his car heavily off the road and into a deep ditch. The accident shook him, and only rarely afterwards was he able to recover his old familiar composure.

A good performance on the Monte Carlo earned him a fifth overall, but at home it seemed that things would never be the same again... And then, with co-driver Stuart Pegg, came that historic second RAC triumph.

"Nice One Albert!" read the headlines in *Motoring News*, eloquently summarizing the mood of the moment. The use of his middle name was by now quite common among reporters, who had become so despondent trying to find something new to say about him that they had taken to combining it with that of Jim Porter to dub the RAC Championship the "Albert and Arnold Show."

"The RAC was one of those events when everything went right," Clark says. "We didn't have any major problems. The car was really quite sophisticated by then, and extremely reliable. We sailed through right from the word go."

There was a brief setback when a bolt worked loose near the end of the rally and the front suspension collapsed. But servicing was a highly efficient business by 1976 and he was quickly back on the road again, beating his nearest rival (Stig Blomqvist, in the new Saab 99EMS) by a margin of more than four minutes.

It was through consistency and determination, rather than out-right speed, that Clark won the RAC that year. After a couple of years of missing out through bad luck, fortune had smiled on him again when it was needed most and might have been expected least.

By far the fastest competitor on the rally was Pentti Airikkala, who had stretched his lead to two and a half minutes before he was booked in just twenty-three seconds late at a time control by co-driver and journalist Mike Greasley. By the rules of the time, that meant disqualification. But the Finn continued under protest in his David Sutton-prepared private Ford Escort until clutch failure left the way clear for Clark.

Despite this second RAC triumph, Clark's halcyon days were drawing to an end. As the advertisements and general media in-terest proved, he was still a most popular figure, but he didn't receive the same recognition as on that first win four years before. Perhaps it was because of his poor record during the season, or perhaps it was the fact that Airikkala had been so much quicker, and that other, newer stars were demanding their share of the headlines, but the end of the year felt like the end of an era.

Clark himself, typically enough, was far from calling it a day. Rallying was more than something he knew and did well and got paid for: it was an activity he enjoyed, and he had no thoughts yet of abandoning it.

Above: A new challenge? Clark had many interests outside rallying, including flying, powerboat racing and circuit racing. History doesn't record his taking up cycling! — Below: Clark had always maintained that he would beat the Porsches on tarmac. On the 1975 Manx, he did just that.

Above: "And you really think we can hide Mason in here, do you?" asks Roger before the start of the 1975 RAC Rally. Below: Spraying the spectators on the RAC in his Cossack Escort. Clark could so easily have won, but mechanical problems saw him finishing second again.

Opposite: Thirsty work, this rallying! Clark swigs a quick coffee before heading off into the forests again.
Above: Another classic Roger Clark shot, this time on the 1976 Welsh Rally.
Below: High hopes. Clark and Stuart Pegg start the 1976 Lombard RAC Rally with an interview.

Above: Grim determination, as Clark tries everything in his power to catch a flying Pentti Airikkala on the '76 RAC.

Below: Sideways again. A calm, steady run was paying off for Clark as Airikkala hit trouble.

RAC champagne again at last! Clark, cameramen and spectators celebrate his second RAC victory.

Above: The works effort abroad continued sporadically for Clark and Ford. This is the 1977 Acropolis Rally.

Below: Clark and Porter pose for the cameras on the '77 Acropolis.

The Autumn Years

Clark still contested the RAC Championship during the late seventies, but never fully recovered the form which had made him so famous and popular. The Escort RS was growing outdated, as four-wheel drive cars became essential equipment. The Escort Mk 2 was soon to be phased out of production altogether, leaving Ford with no good reason for continuing to run it in competition. (As Stuart Turner will point out to anyone who asks, from the manufacturer's viewpoint, rallying serves one purpose only: to sell more cars.)

Ford were concerned to find ways of developing a new model for rallying, and Clark's valuable services were called upon to help with the testing and groundwork. Having become an accomplished test driver over the years, he genuinely enjoyed the work. His mechanical empathy helped him to pinpoint faults, areas for improvement, and, in the case of the latest car in 1978, the total unsuitability of some machines. The car in question was the Ford Fiesta 1600.

"Works rallying at Ford began to fade away quite badly when the Escort was coming to its end. The Fiesta was a total failure in rallying terms. Basically, it had a queer front suspension, which was all right on production models, but no way could you make it work on forest roads. Short of re-designing the car, which regulations didn't allow, there was nothing we could do with it."

It was not a good period for him: "I look on them as wasted years, really," he says, with more than a hint of sadness. Fiestas were entered for Clark and Vatanen on the 1979 Monte Carlo Rally, and while the Finn just scratched his way into the top ten, Clark would sooner forget the experience.

"That was the time when I just sort of faded out of Ford," he says. But why hadn't he moved to another team after that second RAC victory, when Ford's involvement was clearly starting to diminish?

"Well, I'd been with Ford for a long time," he explains. "I was labelled as a Ford man. In those days people didn't change around as much as they do now. And I suppose I'd done most of it, and I was probably losing a bit of enthusiasm."

In 1980, however, Clark found his way into British Leyland, driving a works Triumph TR7 V8. By then, stunning rear-wheel drive supercars were making their mark. (The legendary Lancia Stratos is the most obvious and most spectacular example.) Initially, the TR, with its sports car looks and thundering V8 engine, seemed a viable proposition. Clark joined another great British driver at the team — Tony Pond — and set about contesting the British Championship again.

His move to BL was hardly successful, though. It was a bit of a culture shock in a way: for all its qualities, the Triumph was never going to follow in the Escort's tracks as a rally car. Compared to the handling and agility which had brought him so much success in the past, this new ill-mannered sports car wasn't cut from the same cloth at all.

"Big beasts, short wheel-base, and very twitchy," is Roger's verdict. "But the engine sounded terrific! The fact that you sat much lower in it was also a big handicap in the forests. It wasn't a very successful car, but it was quite good on tarmac: I think Tony Pond won the Manx in it once. It wasn't bad when you could put big fat tyres on it and get some grip. But in the forests, forget it."

Clark was duly entered for the 1980 RAC, alongside Tony Pond, Per Eklund and the American, John Buffum. Hopes rested on them for another home victory, but with over 300 bhp from the V8 engine to tame with unco-operative handling, Clark's personal expectations weren't quite so high. It came as no great surprise, therefore, when the first three places on the rally went to an Escort sandwiched between the Sunbeam Lotuses of Toivonen and Frequelin.

After a change in the rules in 1979 which permitted four-wheel drive for the first time in modern rallying, the writing was on the wall for drivers of Clark's ilk. In March 1980, the Audi Quattro was unveiled: a car which was to revolutionise the sport as the

Escort had done back in 1968. Clark was a generation behind. Not until 1987 would he drive a four-wheel drive supercar of this type (though he did drive a prototype four-wheel drive Sierra for a private team, MCD Services — now Rally Engineering Developments). When the time finally came, it was in circumstances far removed from those barnstorming years in the sixties and seventies, and it was primarily for fun.

Clark continued rallying in Escorts with MCD from time to time, mostly in 1981 in the British Championship and the Lombard RAC Rally, after becoming friendly with the team's boss, Geoff Fielding. His relationship with Fielding led to one of Roger's most famous exploits and again turned him into something of a television star — this time with Chris Serle, for the TV series, *In At The Deep End*.

For those unfamiliar with it, the idea behind the series was that Serle would take part in a number of activities, all requiring varying degrees of skill and daring, which most people with any sense would go out of their way to avoid. Throwing him into a rally car, to co-drive and even drive with Clark, on nothing less than the Lombard RAC Rally, was surely going to be one of his biggest challenges ever? It was — and it provided its startled viewers with a side of Clark's character which rarely surfaces.

As Serle discovered to his cost, Roger Clark does not suffer fools gladly. And while the TV presenter could hardly be described as a fool, the prospect of co-driving on such a major event with only a crash course in navigating was bound to lead to trouble at some stage. Roger laughs heartily about it now, and indeed remembers the incident almost fondly:

"You can't expect someone to be thrown into an international rally, and perform like a pro. Basically I had to do the two jobs of driving and co-driving: not the best of situations. I'd been spoilt over the years by always having very good co-drivers like Jim, Tony, Brian, Stuart and so forth, and here I was having to check every decision."

The most memorable occasion in the programme was after an incident when Serle got lost on a motorway. With little fuel left,

Above: 1977 marked the beginning of the end of Clark's best years at Ford. Here he contests the Lindisfarne National Championship qualifier in a David Sutton-prepared car. — Below: Clark still put in energetic performances on home international rallies such as the 1978 Scottish, where he finished third.

Above: By 1978, Clark was driving mainly on home events in the Li-Lo (waterbeds) Escort RS, but his days of dominating these events were over. He finished fourth on the Mintex. — Below: On tarmac, the Escort was still as competitive as ever, but Clark managed only fourth on the 1978 Circuit of Ireland Rally.

Above: Clark's only major rally in the Fiesta was the 1979 Monte Carlo, but the machine was never going to be competitive. — Below: Roger finally made the break from Ford in 1980 and drove for British Leyland on home internationals in the TR7 V8. On gravel events like the Mintex, he found it a difficult car to drive.

and the prospect of a long drive to the next junction before turning back in the right direction, Roger came as close as is possible for him to losing his temper. And his disgust, too intense and spontaneous to conceal, was on show to millions.

"It was a bit hairy," he laughs. "We got round it all right, no problem, but it didn't do a lot for the enjoyment of the day!... Considering how little he knew, Chris made a pretty good stab at it. It wasn't enjoyable for me, though, because I couldn't concentrate on my driving. But it made good television, I think; a bit of anxiety here and there, instead of the usual bland stuff...

"The television people wanted Chris to drive on a stage, so we gave him Donington Park, which was about the shortest and the least dangerous. He was all right; he was safe, which was the main thing. He'll never be a driver, but he knows that and accepts it. Given the task, he did very well. I mean, a works Escort on gravel for the first time isn't the easiest thing to get used to!"

Clark's interest was revived briefly when he had the opportunity to drive a Porsche. This was a car which Roger had often longed to get his hands on. He had for some time been a Porsche fan, a fact borne out by his owning a Porsche dealership, and his career nearly blossomed again, with talk of a new car and a full programme.

Porsche's plan as he recalls it was to run Clark in the British Championship: "We went to Stuttgart to have a look and to talk to people. But there was a problem: they had no rally equipment for the cars. We were talking about rallying a 944 at the time, but they'd only got a limited amount of race-spec stuff, and the time and cost to develop the 944 for a single car for British events only would have been totally unjustifiable. It was a shame, because it could have been quite something."

His connections with Porsche led to another drive offer in 1984, this time in the 911. David Richards, who had masterminded Vatanen's career in the Rothmans Escorts as his co-driver (and won the World Championship with the Finn in 1981), was running 911s for Rothmans and contacted Clark to drive for the team on the Lombard RAC. Tarmac rallies such as the Donegal and

Manx were included, events to which the car was much more suited than the RAC, surely? Clark agrees:

"On tarmac the Porsche was an exceptionally good car. There was so much torque and traction, and good brakes as well. It was designed as a fast car, whereas the Escort was basically a modified tin box. But in the forests, the Porsche was a dog. It was a real tail-heavy brute, and on mud and other slippery ground, you just didn't know where you were with it."

After the Porsche outings, Clark finally retired. Well, almost: you can never keep a good rally driver down! Apart from "odd bits and bobs" as he describes them, it wasn't until 1986 that his name unexpectedly returned to the headlines.

The occasion was a Pirelli press conference in London's popular restaurant, *L'Escargot,* and the news, to put it mildly, was startling. Clark was making a comeback. Backed by Pirelli, SMC and RED (Geoff Fielding again), he was to contest the National Championship in a Metro 6R4.

By then, of course, the Championship was nothing like the series which Clark had dominated in his heyday. True, some of the rallies were the same, but international events such as the Circuit, Scottish, and Welsh now formed part of the British Open series, while the one-day National rallies existed as a lower echelon for British drivers only. Added to which, the excitement of Clark in a modern day supercar was dulled slightly by their having been banned from international competition at the end of the previous year and being allowed in the British National series only in a somewhat de-tuned form.

It was big news nonetheless, and we were to discover in 1987 that despite the years of inactivity — and the physical signs of a comfortable life! — Clark had lost little of his touch. The season started well for him, even though he had little to prove and one supposes that took the edge off his competitiveness. Quite simply, we were watching a man who enjoyed driving a top class rally car — no big ambitions maybe, and he never really outgunned the opposition the way he used to, but he was still exciting to watch.

Fifth on the National Winter Rally, the first round of the

Above: BL offered hope to British spectators on the 1980 Lombard RAC Rally, with both Clark and Tony Pond in the team. Unfortunately, Clark retired with engine failure when the oil pump pulley failed. — Below: In 1981, Roger developed a relationship with Geoff Fielding and MCD (later RED) and drove one of the team's Escorts.

*Above: Clark and Chris Serle competing together on the 1981 RAC Rally for the TV programme, **In At The Deep End**. It was not a "fun" experience! — Below: With a Porsche dealership near Leicester, it was inevitable that at some time Clark would drive one of the German cars. His popularity demanded that an in-car camera be fitted.*

championship, boded well. But maybe he *was* getting ambitious, after all. As someone noted at the time: "The old man has registered for points!"

Any hopes of winning the series went up literally in flames on the next rally, the Skip Brown, when the Metro developed an electrical fault and started a small fire. But on the Granite City Rally, the scene of so many past victories, Clark again came in fifth.

The Kayel Graphics and Shell Oils Cumbria rallies brought his best results of the season — second on both — and the year finished in creditable style with a sound sixth on the final round of the series, the Audi Sport Rally.

It was hardly the glittering stuff he had given us at his peak. But at least the younger generation had had the benefit of seeing the great man in action, and for Clark himself, there were absolutely no regrets at all:

"The Metro drive was Geoff (Fielding's) idea," he says. "And since I'd never driven a Group B car, it seemed like a fun thing to do… which it was. I really enjoyed it; it was a good season."

SMC and Pirelli must have done quite well out of it too. A year later, Clark came out top in a poll conducted by Ford which found that, more than a decade after his greatest triumphs, he was (and probably still is) the country's most famous rally driver ever. Ironically, at the very same Ford press conference where this poll result was announced, Stuart Turner defended his decision not to hire British drivers, preferring Scandinavians and the new breed of Latin drivers emerging. It sounded all so familiar!

Clark still competes on fun events like the Pirelli Classic Marathon, which runs through the Alps and recreates rallying's good old days. Usually, too, he takes along his old friend Tony Mason, the man with whom he achieved his first historic RAC victory.

For many who witnessed his career, whether before, during or after his peak, rallying without Roger Clark is like cricket without Botham or boxing without Ali. It just isn't the same. But for once, as will be seen in our next chapter, the name literally lives on…

Above: With the Rothmans Porsche team, managed by ex-world champion co-driver David Richards, Roger contested his last RAC Rally in 1984 and finished eleventh. — Below: RED developed this turbocharged four-wheel drive Sierra and hired Roger to drive it in 1985.

Above: 1987 was Roger Clark's last full year in rallying. Here he makes full use of the Metro 6R4's four-wheel drive on a snowy Skip Brown Rally. — Below: Still enjoying himself, Clark shares a laugh with Pirelli man Paul Kendrick (left) and RED Team Manager Peter Cattanach during the Metro year.

Above: Matthew sits on his father's knee in one of the top Ford rally cars of the time. These days he sits behind the wheel. — Below: Matthew's first birthday. Spot the racing car on the cake — who said he wasn't influenced by his father!

THE UNDERGRADUATE

Matthew Clark, at barely 20 years old, is already following in his father's footsteps. And Roger, like any other good father, is standing in the wings, advising, prompting a little, and handing out encouragement.

"I'm not bothered about driving myself any more," he shrugs. "I get as much of a kick now out of seeing Matthew finding his feet" — words which can't conceal his understandable pleasure and pride in Matthew's achievements.

Mindful of the dangers of trying to push his son too fast, Roger kept well out of the way to begin with. Matthew's chief encouragement at the outset came from John Robinson, Roger's co-driver in the Metro 6R4.

On his first rally, Matthew drove a self-built Fiesta XR2 — an ironic choice, in view of his father's verdict on the Fiesta a few years earlier. The event was the Newtown Stages Rally of 1988 and, with Robinson co-driving, young Clark managed a useful 34th place. Even so, the Fiesta was soon exchanged for a Group A (modified saloon) Peugeot 205GTI, built with the assistance of Chartersport's Tony Cox.

It wasn't long before Matthew found himself among the front runners in his class in the National Championships. His most promising performance that year was on the Quip National Rally, when he led his class before puncturing a tyre, and this was bettered the following year on the Vauxhall Sport Rally: eighteenth overall, and second in class.

Matthew was also studying long hours for qualifications in mechanical engineering. This brought him into contact with David Sutton, who for many years had been preparing some of the best rally cars in Britain, particularly Fords. For the Manx Rally of 1990, young Clark managed to borrow a Sutton Sierra Cosworth from his new employer, and within just a few stages we all knew that he had inherited at least some of his father's talent.

Above: The family together at home at the time of the Fiesta launch in 1978/79.

Below: Matthew (with brother Oliver) getting behind the wheel at an early age.

Matthew was lying fourth overall — an almost incredible achievement for someone with so little experience of such a powerful car — and must have been hoping for his first really big result. Sadly, it was not to be. Two punctures robbed him of vital time, ending his effort in anti-climactic retirement.

Clark Sr. was impressed: "To get into that position first time out on the Manx is a bit serious," was his pleased, but typically understated, comment.

In recent years, there have been several "motorsport sons" announcing their intentions to emulate (and perhaps even outdo) their famous fathers. Not all have lived up to the family reputation. In rallying, Jim McRae's son, Colin, has so far been the most successful, indicating at times that he might be even faster than Dad. Roger Clark, wisely, is prepared to wait and see.

"Whether he's going to win anything is too early to say, at this stage. But he's certainly showing he's got the ability… Since he was fourteen or fifteen, he's been autocrossing and so on — he just loves motor cars.

"He's doing a broad spectrum of events," Roger continues, "and he's built just about everything himself. All I've done is give him a written-off car and a shell and told him to go off and play with it!"

This apart, Roger's involvement stretches to following his son around with Judith in a Range Rover, helping out with servicing if needs be, and generally "keeping an eye on things". (He is also keeping an eye on younger son Oliver, who has passed his test and is "very interested in driving", though still too young to have committed himself to any form of competition.)

Matthew provided further evidence of his promise on the 1990 Donegal Rally. He was lying in the top ten of this very specialised event, when the car left the road following a confusion over the pace notes and got itself stuck in a bog.

"The Sutton Sierra has been a lot of fun for him," Roger maintains. "It's the first time he's driven left-hand drive and the first time with 300-odd horsepower, so he's really acquitted himself well."

While Matthew just begins his career, Dad has been keeping his hand in with historic events such as the Pirelli Classic marathon. In 1989 he drove a Mk 1 Lotus Cortina.

Tuition in driving techniques has never been forthcoming from Roger, at least not in any formal sense. "If he needs my experience, he's just not going to get there. I believe a driver is someone who's born, not made."

Recently, Matthew was selected by Ford as one of the "trainees" in the Group N (standard class) Sierra Sapphire Cosworth 4x4 programme. Drivers chosen for this scheme can recoup the cost of converting a standard car into a rally machine by agreeing to compete in at least three British Open Championship rallies. It's one of the most likely routes to a works drive with Ford, and the best driver at the end of the year earns himself a substantial contribution towards contesting a World Championship rally.

Regardless of its outcome, simply to have been chosen by Ford is an achievement of which both father and son are understandably proud.

Matthew clearly has the will, the skill and the opportunity to succeed and the early stages of the two Clarks' careers reveal some remarkable, maybe prophetic, parallels.

One Clark to remember; another to watch. And, even if Matthew never quite sets the world alight as his legendary father did, perhaps in a decade or so there'll be another great success story to tell. Nothing, you can be sure, could bring Roger greater happiness.

Above: Matthew Clark certainly hasn't come to rallying with "a silver spoon in his mouth". The Fiesta he is driving here on the Severn Rally was built by himself as part of a college project. (Nick Ford)

Below: Matthew progressed quickly to a Peugeot 205GTI and, while he suffered a degree of ill-luck, managed to impress many in his class on national events such as the 1989 Cumbria.

Two fine action shots of Matthew on the 1990 Manx Rally. A double puncture forced him to retire when lying fourth overall in his first event in a Sierra Cosworth.
(Speedsports Photography)

"PURE MAGIC..."

Thoughts and recollections of Roger Clark, by co-driver and friend, Tony Mason.

THE EARLY DAYS

I first met Roger in the early sixties. We were on the Shunpiker Rally, a very tough road rally in Wales which started from Blackpool and the Midlands and finished in Chester. Roger started just behind us in his red Mini-Cooper and I remember him overtaking us on a narrow Welsh moorland road as though jet-propelled. I spoke to him for the first time after breakfast. He wasn't too talkative, having wrong slotted a few times during the night and consequently not managing a very good result.

A few weekends later, he was back in action on a snowy Welsh Marches Rally. Most of the top cars were running on fairly crude studded tyres — Durabands. There was an award for the best non-studded performance and the red Mini-Cooper of one R. Clark carried off this trophy. He was actually placed third or fourth overall — an astonishing performance.

We met frequently on club rallies, but Roger never did particularly well. I felt that he probably went too quickly for his navigators, as all these rallies called for highly intricate map-reading. One night, Frank Grange, a regular member of the rally circus, and I retired with engine trouble on a London Rally in mid-Wales. We parked up to watch the cars drive down a steep muddy section and through a rutted gateway. The top drivers of the day treated it with some respect and gingerly negotiated the narrow opening. Suddenly there were spotlight beams coming considerably quicker than anything that had gone before. It was a red Cortina, reg. 2 ANR, and it careered down the track and through the gate at literally twice the speed of anything else. Frank and I could hardly believe what we had seen.

In the late sixties, Roger entered the Players No. 6 Autocross Championship in a Mk 2 Lotus Cortina. These were super social affairs over the length and breadth of Britain. Roger and Goo would drive from Leicester to the meetings towing the car on a trailer. Needless to say, Roger won his class every time, taking lines round grass fields that no-one else dared. He would often beat the four-wheel drive Autocross specials. He was sponsored by Calypso cigars at one point, and I remember a front wheel coming adrift. Clark kept going full bore, of course, and finished on three wheels. We called it the "Collapso" Cortina thereafter.

I used to enter my Cooper S in those days, and several fellow Morecambe Car Club members competed. After the event, we'd all make for the nearest pub with the Clarks and their friends, and in those glorious pre-breathalyser times we'd spend a pleasant Sunday evening till chucking-out time when we'd all head for home.

We formed a close friendship, and when I became involved with Ford in the early seventies I would stay with Roger and Goo in their house in Hinckley prior to going to the Jim Russell Racing Drivers' School at Mallory Park. Ford team boss Stuart Turner thought it was a good idea for co-drivers to be competent behind the wheel as well, so I was duly despatched on a six-month course. Roger thought it very funny that Turner should send me to learn how to drive him while he was sleeping, for this was to become my role on many rallies. Roger was the laziest of drivers and would jump into the passenger seat at the end of practically every stage and promptly fall asleep. Sometimes he would just sit and navigate. I would drive him (expertly — thanks to Jim Russell!) to the next stage where he would transfer to the driving seat and set forth on the test. I have been known to drive as much as 75% of the road sections!

OUR FIRST RALLY

My first rally with Roger was the 1972 Seven Dales (later the Mintex, National Breakdown, Cartel…!). In those days, it was a two days and a night non-stop. The days were stages and the night was a road rally in North Yorkshire and the Lake District. To sit alongside this amazing driver and suddenly see a whole new method of car control was unforgettable. On the muddy, rutted tracks over the moors, he would appear to pick the car up and aim it through the ruts. We had a huge lead by the time the night rally started.

I was obviously nervous, feeling that the eyes of British and certainly all local rally enthusiasts were on me. Map reading was difficult, but I was the local champion (which was probably why Stuart Turner had put me in the seat) and thankfully I never put a foot wrong. I remember going down well-known roads which I frequently used on club rallies and where I knew the quickest possible time to the second. I'd been with many good road rally drivers over one section in particular, which I "knew" could not be completed in less than twelve minutes. Roger, having never seen it in his life, did it in *ten minutes* and a few seconds!

By the end of the rally, we had increased our lead to thirteen minutes and won. I believe that this is a record winning margin for a national rally. It was also the last national rally to include a night navigation section. Incidentally, we were in a left-hand drive Escort, LVX 941J, which made the procedure at controls very interesting. I'd have to hand my timecard over to Roger and the club marshals would then be completely flustered, never having been so close to the great man. I would then have to lean across to check the time, so I reckon we probably lost about five minutes or so in the night, with all the messing about.

WINNING THE RAC

The RAC win in 1972 was just fantastic, of course. We can still both recall the prize-giving in York and our emotions when the

National Anthem was played. Nor shall we forget the uproarious party held by the Ford team... when Timo Makinen performed his party trick with empty beer bottles, Eric Jackson recited Yorkshire monologues, and Roger and I did our double-act. This consisted of a slim Tony Mason sitting on Roger's knee, playing dummy to his ventriloquist. He had his hand up the back of my jacket and I'd do the exaggerated head movements, periodically falling off his knee to the floor. It was, we're told, extremely funny. The act was first conceived with the then Dunlop PR man Ian Norris, after a Ford forum in Hull, and was the one and only time that Stuart Turner was seen to cry with laughter.

The rest of the night is something of a blur. We visited every nightclub in York and never bought a drink all night — or for several months after, for that matter!

The RAC win changed my life completely, as I was relatively unknown before that and was now suddenly the co-driver of a household name. We spent our entire time going to dinners, receptions, TV and radio studios, and we visited practically every Ford dealer in Britain. We also managed to win a few more rallies together and spend a heck of a lot of time in each other's company.

It's difficult to describe the euphoria after that one and only all-British win. We received letters and cards from hundreds of fans, and we would appear at motor club evenings where there were queues lining the street and over six hundred people present. We came back to earth at one such meeting in a small Welsh border town, where the ancient club member taking tickets at the door didn't recognise us and charged us to get in!

ROGER'S MANAGER

During my time with Ford as Competitions Co-ordinator, I suppose I became Roger's boss to some extent. I still co-drove for him occasionally and we managed two second places on the RAC. We remained close friends and would see a lot of each other socially, but I then acquired yet another respect for him — that of team member and tester. He was an extremely able test driver. I did many, many laps of Bagshot with him, evaluating everything from engines to suspension.

COSSACK

It was in Bagshot that we filmed the famous Cossack Hairspray commercial. The film people hadn't a clue and made an artificial jump just fifty yards before a T junction. So Roger told them to re-site it, which several hours later they did. Before filming, we indicated where he might land. The director wouldn't believe it and promptly focused his camera five yards after the jump. It scarcely needs saying that on his first run Roger passed virtually over the top of the camera and landed, just where he said he would, twenty yards along the track!

One especially amusing memory is of a rude early morning awakening Roger received. Having shared hundreds of rooms with Roger all over the world, I know his sleeping habits well. Never one to waken easily, he is a far from pretty sight first thing — especially the morning after the night before. He was woken this particular morning when a young, effeminate male hair- dresser was sent into the room at 6.00 am to shampoo and cut his hair for the commercial. I can remember to this day the bleary-eyed Clark hunched up on the end of the bed while the hair-dresser scurried and fussed with his scissors and blow-dryer. Roger was not amused.

OUR NEW PARTNERSHIP

Though we didn't see a lot of each other in the late seventies and eighties when I left the rallying scene to concentrate on my business, we were reunited by Bob Newman of Pirelli who thought it would be a good idea to put us together in a Lotus Cortina for the second Pirelli Classic Marathon. We met up at Boreham to check the car over and it was as if we'd never been separated. We got on like a house on fire, and we had a marvellous time on the rally, even though the car let us down. Sitting next to Roger felt exactly the same as it had always done — pure magic, as he displayed all his old skills.

We've since done various things together, and enjoyed each other's company both on the events and after them. On the Pirelli Classic, Stirling Moss thinks we're quite unprofessional in our late-night carousing. We reckon that's what we used to do when we were on "proper" rallies, so why not now?

Roger is a quiet, introvert person and many people wonder how I can spend a week or more with him when he says so little. In truth, I cannot say I've found it a problem. We chat happily about all sorts of things and I very much enjoy his company.

Jim Porter is another quiet chap, of course, so I imagine that many, many miles went by in those days without a word being spoken. But, as the records show, it didn't prevent them from being a brilliant combination.

MATTHEW CLARK

My view is that Matthew will be a truly outstanding rally driver, in the same mould as his father. Roger has started him off properly and doesn't want him trying to run before he can walk. Nor does he want him to be seen as one of the "silver spoon" brigade. Matthew is learning about the mechanics, starting with low-powered cars and moving on at a planned pace.

Although I've never sat in a car with Matthew, I can see that he has inherited some of Roger's habits. He sits in the seat the same way, he stretches his neck towards the windscreen during the final countdown to a special stage start, and displays that same controlled aggression. He's a super young man, and very modest. He's not quite as shy as his father and is already working on his media personality. He will be a great star, I'm sure.

Best of friends. Tony Mason and Roger Clark after the 1990 Pirelli Classic. Looks like another marathon is getting under way!

I remember seeing young Matthew at two playing with his first toy cars and looking at his father's rally car photos. I thought then that he was a chip off the old block. I've known him since he was a few months old — not quite as young as his younger brother Oliver was when I first saw him, though. I saw Oliver the day he was born and, by special arrangement, took a Polaroid photo of him before setting off to Kenya where I was to join Roger on recce for the Safari. I arrived at the Norfolk Hotel, Nairobi, handed over letters and notes from Goo and proudly presented my photograph of his new son and heir. "Isn't he pink!" Roger exclaimed. We had a few jokes about it probably being my thumb over the lens; and then, with Roger's close friend Bill Parkinson, one of the funniest men in the world, we started to celebrate!

RESULTS TABLES 1961 - 1990

Event	Co-driver	Car	Result	Comments
1961				
Circuit of Ireland	J. Porter	Renault Dauphine	51st, Class 12th	
RAC	J. Porter, J. Oldham	850 Mini	52nd	
1962				
Circuit of Ireland	J. Porter	Mini-Cooper	4th, Class 1st	
Scottish	R. Marriott	Mini-Cooper	Nowhere	Navigational error
London	J. Porter	Mini-Cooper	14th	
RAC	J. Porter	Mini-Cooper	Retired	
1963				
Express and Star	J. Porter	Mini-Cooper	Retired	Driveshaft failure
Birmingham Post	J. Porter	Mini-Cooper	Retired	Lost transmission plug
Circuit of Ireland	J. Porter	Mini-Cooper	Retired	Clutch failure
Tulip Rally	J. Oldham	Mini-Cooper	Retired	
Scottish	H. Patton	Mini-Cooper	2nd	
Coupe des Alpes	R. Aston	Reliant Sabre Six	6th GT, Class 2nd	
Liege-Sofia-Liege	B. Culcheth	Triumph TR4	Retired	Fractured exhaust, seized gearbox
RAC	J. Porter	Mini-Cooper	Retired	Gearbox failure
1964				
Welsh	J. Porter	Mini-Cooper	Retired	Gearbox failure
Express and Star	J. Porter	Cortina GT	3rd	
Circuit of Ireland	J. Porter	Cortina GT	Retired	Dynamo failure
Acropolis	R. Martin-Hurst	Rover 3-litre	9th	
Scottish	J. Porter	Cortina GT	1st	
Coupe des Alpes	J. Syer	Rover 2000	Retired	Axle failure
Rally of the Vales	J. Porter	Cortina GT	20th	
Liege-Sofia-Liege	B. Culcheth	Rover 2000	Retired	Gearbox failure
Gulf London	J. Porter	Cortina GT	Retired	
RAC	J. Porter	Rover 2000	Retired	Engine failure
1965				
Welsh	J. Porter	Cortina GT	Retired	Broken spring
Monte Carlo	J. Porter	Rover 2000	6th, Class 1st	
Express and Star	J. Porter	Rover 2000	Retired	Diff. failure
Circuit of Ireland	J. Porter	Cortina GT	3rd	
Tulip Rally	B. Melia	Cortina GT	Retired	Engine and electrics
Acropolis	J. Porter	Rover 2000	Retired	Accident
Scottish	J. Porter	Cortina GT	1st	
Gulf London	J. Porter	Cortina GT	1st	

Coupe des Alpes	J. Porter	Rover 2000	10th	
RAC	J. Porter	Rover 2000	14th, Class 2nd	
Welsh	G. Robson	Lotus-Cortina	1st	

1966

Monte Carlo	B. Melia	Lotus-Cortina	Disqualified	
Circuit of Ireland	J. Porter	Lotus-Cortina	Retired	Oil pump failure
Shell 4000	R. Edwardes	Lotus-Cortina	3rd	
Acropolis	B. Melia	Lotus-Cortina	2nd	
Scottish	B. Melia	Lotus-Cortina	Retired	Diff. failure
Gulf London	J. Porter	Lotus-Cortina	Retired	Diff. failure
Polish	B. Melia	Lotus-Cortina	4th	
1000 Lakes	B. Melia	Lotus-Cortina	19th	
Coupe des Alpes	B. Melia	Lotus-Cortina	2nd	
RAC	J. Porter	Lotus-Cortina	Retired	Accident
Welsh	J. Porter	Lotus-Cortina	Retired	Accident

1967

Monte Carlo	J. Porter	Ford Taunus 20M	67th	
East African Safari	G. Staepelaere	Lotus-Cortina	Nowhere	
Shell 4000	J. Peters	Lotus-Cortina Mk 2	1st	
Scottish	J. Porter	Lotus-Cortina Mk 2	1st	
Gulf London	J. Porter	Lotus-Cortina Mk 2	Retired	Broken engine oil pipe

1968

Swedish	J. Porter	Lotus-Cortina Mk 2	Retired	Unwell
Circuit of Ireland	J. Porter	Escort Twin-Cam	1st	
Tulip Rally	J. Porter	Escort Twin-Cam	1st	
Acropolis	J. Porter	Escort Twin-Cam	1st	
Scottish	J. Porter	Escort Twin-Cam	1st	
Coupe des Alpes	J. Porter	Escort Twin-Cam	Retired	Accident
London-Sydney Marathon	O. Andersson	Lotus-Cortina	10th	

1969

San Remo	J. Porter	Escort Twin-Cam	10th	
Circuit of Ireland	J. Porter	Escort Twin-Cam	1st	
Acropolis	J. Porter	Escort Twin-Cam	2nd	
Scottish	J. Porter	Escort Twin-Cam	Retired	Broken suspension strut
Coupe des Alpes	J. Porter	Escort V6 2.3	Retired	Overheating
Three Cities	J. Porter	Zodiac Mk 4	16th, Class 1st	
RAC	J. Porter	Escort Twin-Cam	6th	

1970

Smile Rally	C. Freud	Escort Twin-Cam	5th	
Monte Carlo	J. Porter	Escort Twin-Cam	5th, Class 1st	
Circuit of Ireland	J. Porter	Escort RS1600	1st	
World Cup London-Mexico	A. Poole	Escort 1800	Retired	Accident
Scottish	J. Porter	Escort RS1600	Retired	Engine failure

Jamaica 1000	—	Cortina GT	Retired	Navigational error
TAP	J. Porter	Escort RS1600	Retired	Engine failure
RAC	J. Porter	Escort RS1600	Retired	Half-shaft failure

1971

East African Safari	G. Staepelaere	Escort Twin-Cam	Retired	
Granite City	H. Cardno	Escort RS1600	1st	
Welsh	G. Phillips	Escort RS1600	Retired	Diff. failure
Hackle	J. Porter	Escort RS1600 1st		
Ronde Cevenole	—	GT70	Retired	Engine failure
Manx	H. Liddon	Escort RS1600	1st	
RAC	J. Porter	Escort RS1600	11th	

1972

Snowman	H. Cardno	Escort RS1600	Retired	Accident
Seven Dales	A. Mason	Escort RS1600	1st	
Hong Kong	J. Porter	Escort RS1600	2nd	
Granite City	J. Porter	Escort RS1600	1st	
Welsh	J. Porter	Escort RS1600	1st	
Scottish	J. Porter	Escort RS1600	2nd	
Jim Clark	J. Porter	Escort RS1600	1st	
Burmah	J. Porter	Escort RS1600	1st	
Manx	J. Porter	Escort RS1600	1st	
Lindisfarne	J. Porter	Escort RS1600	Retired	Wheel off
Dukeries	J. Porter	Escort RS1600	1st	
Hackle	J. Porter	Escort RS1600	1st	
RAC	A. Mason	Escort RS1600	1st	

1973

Snowman	J. Porter	Escort RS1600	1st	
Mintex Dales	J. Porter	Escort RS1600	1st	
East African Safari	J. Porter	Escort RS1600	Retired	Alternator burnt out
Granite City	J. Porter	Escort RS1600	1st	
Welsh	J. Porter	Escort RS1600	1st	
Scottish	J. Porter	Escort RS1600	1st	
Jim Clark	A. Mason	Escort RS1600	1st	
Tour of Britain	A. Mason	Capri 3-litre	Retired	Electrics failure
Hackle	J. Porter	Escort RS1600	1st	
Burmah	J. Porter	Escort RS1500	1st	
Manx	J. Porter	Escort RS1600	Retired	Engine failure
Dukeries	J. Porter	Escort RS1600	1st	
Lindisfarne	J. Porter	Escort RS1600	1st	
RAC	A. Mason	Escort RS1600	2nd	

1974

Welsh	J. Porter	Escort RS1600	Retired	Blown head gasket
Jim Clark	J. Porter	Escort RS1600	1st	
Tour of Britain	J. Porter	Escort RS2000	1st	

Burmah	J. Porter	Escort RS1600	41st	Timing error
Total	A. Mason	Escort RS1600	Retired	Clutch failure
Manx	J. Porter	Escort RS1600	3rd	
Dukeries	J. Porter	Escort RS1600	Retired	
Lindisfarne	J. Porter	Escort RS1600	1st	
RAC	A. Mason	Escort RS1600	7th	

1975

Mintex Dales	J. Porter	Escort RS1600	Retired	Engine failure
Circuit of Ireland	J. Porter	Escort RS1600	Retired	Engine failure
Granite City	J. Porter	Escort RS1800	1st	
Welsh	J. Porter	Escort RS1800	1st	
Scottish	J. Porter	Escort RS1800	1st	
Antibes	J. Porter	Escort RS1800	Retired	Suspension failure
Jim Clark	J. Porter	Escort RS1800	Retired	Accident
South African Total	S. Pegg	Escort RS1800	1st	
Burmah	J. Porter	Escort RS1800	1st	
Manx	J. Porter	Escort RS1800	1st	
San Remo	J. Porter	Escort RS1800	Retired	Tyres worn out
Lindisfarne	J. Porter	Escort RS1800	1st	
RAC	A. Mason	Escort RS1800	2nd	

1976

Shellsport Dean	J. Porter	Escort RS1800	1st	
Monte Carlo	J. Porter	Escort RS1800	5th	
Snowman	J. Porter	Escort RS1800	2nd	
Mintex	J. Porter	Escort RS1800	Retired	Accident
Granite City	J. Porter	Escort RS1800	2nd	
Firestone	J. Porter	Escort RS1800	Retired	Blown head gasket
Welsh	J. Porter	Escort RS1800	3rd	
Scottish	J. Porter	Escort RS1800	2nd	
Morocco	J. Porter	Escort RS1800	Retired	Seized camshaft
Jim Clark	J. Porter	Escort RS1800	3rd	
Texaco Tour of Britain	J. Porter	Escort RS2000	Retired	Clutch failure
South African Total	S. Pegg	Escort RS1800	2nd	
Burmah	J. Porter	Escort RS1800	2nd	
Ulster	J. Porter	Escort RS1800	Retired	Broken throttle linkage
Manx Trophy	J. Porter	Escort RS1800	Retired	Accident
Southern Cross	J. Porter	Escort RS1800	Nowhere	
Wyedean	M. Greasley	Escort RS1800	2nd	
RAC	S. Pegg	Escort RS1800	1st	

1977

Galway	J. Porter	Escort RS1800	1st	
Portugese	J. Porter	Escort RS1800	Retired	Clutch failure
Safari	J. Porter	Escort RS1800	Retired	Engine failure
Acropolis	J. Porter	Escort RS1800	2nd	
Circuit of Donegal	J. Porter	Escort RS1800	Retired	Blown head gasket

South African Total	J. Porter	Escort RS1800	Retired	Clutch failure
Critérium de Québec	J. Porter	Escort RS1800	3rd	
Lindisfarne	J. Porter	Escort RS1800	Retired	Engine failure
RAC	S. Pegg	Escort RS1800	4th	

1978

Mintex	J. Porter	Escort RS1800	4th	
Circuit of Ireland	J. Porter	Escort RS1800	4th	
Welsh	J. Porter	Escort RS1800	2nd	
Scottish	J. Porter	Escort RS1800	3rd	
Burmah	J. Porter	Escort RS1800	3rd	
Manx	J. Porter	Escort RS1800	4th	
Cyprus	J. Porter	Escort RS1800	1st	
RAC	N. Wilson	Escort RS1800	Retired	Accident/mechanical failure

1979

Monte Carlo	J. Porter	Fiesta	Nowhere	
West Cork	J. Porter	Fiesta	9th	
Plains	J. Porter	Fiesta	Retired	Engine failure
Circuit of Ireland	J. Porter	Fiesta	Retired	Engine failure
Welsh	J. Porter	Fiesta	20th	
Acropolis	J. Porter	Escort RS1800	Retired	Blown head gasket
Scottish	J. Porter	Fiesta	Nowhere	
Mopar Manx Int.	J. Porter	Fiesta	Retired	Clutch failure
RAC	N. Wilson	Escort RS1800	Retired	Engine failure

1980

Galway	J. Porter	Triumph TR7 V8	Retired	Engine failure
Mintex	J. Porter	Triumph TR7 V8	Retired	Engine failure
Circuit of Ireland	J. Porter	Triumph TR7 V8	Retired	Engine failure
Atcost 80 Int.	J. Porter	Triumph TR7 V8	Retired	Oil pump
Scottish	J. Porter	Triumph TR7 V8	9th	
Manx	J. Porter	Triumph TR7 V8	Retired	Transmission failure
Cyprus	N. Wilson	Escort RS1800	1st	
RAC	N. Wilson	Triumph TR7 V8	Retired	Engine failure

1981

Welsh	J. Porter	Escort RS1800	Retired	Gearbox failure
Manx	J. Porter	Escort RS1800	5th	
Pace National	C. Serle	Escort RS1800	5th	
RAC	C. Serle	Escort RS1800	10th	

1982

No events contested

1983

No events contested

1984

Donegal	E. Morgan	RED T 4x4	Retired	Engine failure
RAC	I. Grindrod	Porsche 911 SLRS	11th	

1985

Gwynedd	J. Robinson	RED 4 T 4x4	3rd

1986

No events contested

1987

Citroen Winter	J. Robinson	MG Metro 6R4	5th	
Skip Brown	J. Robinson	MG Metro 6R4	Retired	Engine failure
Granite City	J. Robinson	MG Metro 6R4	5th	
Manx	J. Robinson	MG Metro 6R4	Nowhere	
Kayel Graphics	J. Robinson	MG Metro 6R4	2nd	
Cumbria	J. Robinson	MG Metro 6R4	2nd	
Quip Stages	J. Robinson	MG Metro 6R4	7th	
Audi Sport	J. Robinson	MG Metro 6R4	6th	

1988

No events contested

1989

Pirelli Classic Marathon	A. Mason	Lotus Cortina Mk 1	20th
Tour of Britain	D. Smith	Ford Sierra Cosworth	4th

1990

Pirelli Classic Marathon	A. Mason	MGB	7th
Manx Historic	A. Poole	Mini Cooper S	3rd

Unforgettable. December 1972, and Roger Clark and co-driver Tony Mason sit triumphantly atop LVX 942J as winners of the 1972 RAC Rally. For those who were there and watching, the memory is priceless.

David Campbell started his writing career as a freelance journalist in his home town of Lisburn, Northern Ireland, covering local motor-sport events for regional daily newspapers. Early in 1986 he moved to London where he spent two years as Assistant Rallies Editor on *Motoring News* before taking up his present position as Editor of *Rally Car*. He has wide experience of rallying, having covered events for both magazines all over the world, and he competes regularly on rallies as a co-driver and, occasionally, driver.

David is married to Amanda and lives in Gloucestershire. This is his first book.